F Horn

T0081904

Great Hymns

Instrumental Solos for Worship

Contents

CURNOW® MUSIC

Arranged by James Curnow

Great Hymns

INTRODUCTION

This collection of some of the world's greatest hymns was created for, and is dedicated to, my good friend and musical colleague, Philip Smith, Principal Trumpet, New York Philharmonic Orchestra. The goal of these arrangements is to allow instrumentalists the opportunity to give praise and adoration to God through their musical abilities.

Though the arrangements have been written for trumpet, with Phil in mind, cued notes have been added to allow players at many different levels and on various instruments to perform them. They are also playable on all instruments (C treble clef, Bb Treble Clef, Eb, F or Bass Clef) by simply purchasing the appropriate book that coincides with the key of their instrument.

The piano accompaniment book has been written to work with all instruments or an accompaniment track for each hymn is included on the compact disc, should a piano accompanist not be available. Appropriate tuning notes have also been added to the compact disc recording to allow the soloists the opportunity to adjust their intonation to the intonation of the compact disc accompaniment.

May you enjoy using this collection and find it useful in extending your musical ministry.

Kindest regards,

James Curnow
President
Curnow Music Press, Inc.

Order number: CMP 0351.00
ISBN 90-431-1035-3
NUGI 443
CD number: 19.010-3 CMP *CD performed by Becky Shaw - Piano, Michael Rintamaa - Organ*

James Curnow
Great Hymns
F Horn, E♭ Horn

ALL CREATURES OF OUR GOD AND KING

Track: 2 12

Lasst Uns Erfreuen

Arr. **James Curnow** (ASCAP)

PRAISE TO THE LORD, THE ALMIGHTY

Track: 3 13

Lobe Den Herren

Arr. **James Curnow** (ASCAP)

Track: 4 14

BE THOU MY VISION

Slane

Arr. **James Curnow** (ASCAP)

O WORSHIP THE KING

Track: 5 15

Lyons

Arr. **James Curnow** (ASCAP)

JOYFUL, JOYFUL, WE ADORE THEE

Hymn to Joy

Arr. **James Curnow** (ASCAP)

Track: 6 16

BRETHREN, WE HAVE MET TO WORSHIP

Track: 7 17

Holy Manna Variations

Arr. **James Curnow** (ASCAP)

WE GATHER TOGETHER

Track: 8 18

Kremser

Arr. **James Curnow** (ASCAP)

I SING THE MIGHTY POWER OF GOD

Track: 9 19

Ellacombe

Arr. **James Curnow** (ASCAP)

Track: 10 20

A MIGHTY FORTRESS IS OUR GOD

Ein' Feste Burg

Arr. **James Curnow** (ASCAP)

ALL HAIL THE POWER

Track: 11 21

Coronation, Diadem, Miles Lane

Arr. **James Curnow** (ASCAP)

E♭ Horn

Great Hymns

Instrumental Solos for Worship

Contents

CURNOW® MUSIC

Arranged by James Curnow

ALL CREATURES OF OUR GOD AND KING

Lasst Uns Erfreuen

Arr. **James Curnow** (ASCAP)

Track: 2 12

Edition Number: CMP 0351.00

PRAISE TO THE LORD, THE ALMIGHTY

Track: 3 13

Lobe Den Herren

Arr. **James Curnow** (ASCAP)

P.O. Box 142, Wilmore, KY 40390, USA
Edition Number: CMP 0359.00

BE THOU MY VISION

Slane

Track: 4 14

Arr. **James Curnow** (ASCAP)

O WORSHIP THE KING

Track: 5 15

Lyons

Arr. **James Curnow** (ASCAP)

JOYFUL, JOYFUL, WE ADORE THEE

Track: 6 16

Hymn to Joy

Arr. **James Curnow** (ASCAP)

BRETHREN, WE HAVE MET TO WORSHIP

Track: 7 17

Holy Manna Variations

Arr. **James Curnow** (ASCAP)

WE GATHER TOGETHER

Track: 8 18

Kremser

Arr. **James Curnow** (ASCAP)

I SING THE MIGHTY POWER OF GOD

Track: 9 19

Ellacombe

Arr. **James Curnow** (ASCAP)

Track: 10 20

A MIGHTY FORTRESS IS OUR GOD

Ein' Feste Burg

Arr. **James Curnow** (ASCAP)

Track: 11 21

ALL HAIL THE POWER

Coronation, Diadem, Miles Lane

Arr. **James Curnow** (ASCAP)